# choking the apocalypse

axton seven

copyright © 2025 by axton seven
all rights reserved.

no part of this book may be reproduced or
used in any manner without the
prior written permission of the copyright
owner, except for the use of brief
quotations in a book review.

first edition 2025
isbn 9798305418682 (paperback)

castle keep publishing
cambridge
info@castlekeep.org

**contents**

| | |
|---|---|
| choking the apocalypse | 4 |
| the note | 8 |
| mr grief | 12 |
| the bus ride | 14 |
| my dead dog | 17 |
| the date | 19 |
| old friend | 23 |
| the party hat | 27 |
| the picnic | 30 |
| passing shadows | 34 |
| first day | 38 |
| made her mine | 41 |
| meeting of minds | 43 |
| my tune | 46 |
| mum and dad | 48 |
| i hate you | 50 |
| nativity | 53 |
| stuffed | 56 |
| the playground kings | 59 |
| seaside arcade | 62 |
| flesh sanctuary | 66 |

| | |
|---|---|
| the plan | 68 |
| encounter in aisle five | 71 |
| in translation | 76 |
| the umbrella | 80 |
| the ghost of home | 83 |
| the first sip | 88 |
| before the party | 90 |
| the man in the mirror | 93 |
| the woman in the mirror | 97 |
| unseen | 102 |
| the room you left behind | 105 |
| close call | 109 |
| lost hour | 113 |
| the noise | 116 |
| the old couple | 120 |
| the midnight olympics | 123 |
| a first encounter | 127 |
| the edge of knowing | 130 |
| the inkless author | 134 |

| | |
|---|---|
| what is love? | 137 |
| alternative lives | 139 |
| the babysitter | 141 |
| her, mate | 144 |
| hands | 146 |
| the package | 148 |
| graveyard games | 152 |
| time alone | 155 |
| deathtrap in disguise | 157 |
| sunday roast | 161 |

**Introduction**

Poetry often wears the crown of the extraordinary - a realm of lofty ideals, metaphors, and grand declarations. Yet, some of the most profound poetry thrives not in the celestial but in the terrestrial, in the spaces we all inhabit daily. This collection is rooted in relatability and observation, a celebration of the moments that make up the bulk of our lives: the missed train, the crumpled receipt, the hand you no longer hold. These are the touchstones of shared human experience, where the intimate becomes universal.

Observational poetry, in particular, allows us to hold a mirror to life - not the polished mirror of fantasy but the smudged, scratched mirror of reality. Its philosophy is simple yet profound: that the mundane deserves attention, that beauty, humour, and significance can be found in overlooked corners. This kind of poetry doesn't demand that we transcend the ordinary but invites us to dive into it, to see the patterns, absurdities, and truths beneath the surface.

Relatability in poetry is its bridge. It creates a connection, a moment of recognition: *I've felt this, too.* It allows the reader not just to witness but to step inside the poem, to walk its rhythm and wear its emotions. All poetry has its value, but there is something especially enjoyable about relating to situations that are both familiar and alien in one simultaneous swipe.

This collection invites you to pause, to notice, to find the extraordinary within the familiar and to spot the significance embedded in the insignificance of daily life and mundane routine. It is a map of the small yet magnificent, written in the language of shared experience. It is, above all, an invitation to see yourself within its lines - your laughter, your longing, your unpolished, everyday soul.

## choking the apocalypse

so this is how it ends:
not with a bang,
but a wheeze,
a cough lodged somewhere between
the throat and the soul.

the news anchors gave up hours ago -
their hair, perfect until the bitter end,
their voices dripping with that brand of calm
you save for dying pets.
now it's just static,
or maybe that's the sound of the sky
ripping itself apart.

what do you do when the world's clock
winds down to zero?
boil the kettle, obviously.
there's tea to drink,
biscuits to dip -

might as well go out
with a sugar rush.

the neighbours are arguing again.
apparently, he never fixed the shelf in 2014,
and now it feels like a betrayal
worthy of the apocalypse.
i wonder if i should tell them
that shelves are moot now,
but it feels rude to interrupt.

outside, the horizon glows orange,
like a city made of embers.
someone's car alarm wails -
dedicated to the endgame,
a lone soprano in the orchestra of chaos.
i imagine the person who owns it
pacing in their living room,
thinking, *should i turn it off?*
*does it matter? does anything?*

in the kitchen, i sift through drawers.
what do you pack
for the end of everything?
passport? no borders left to cross.
phone? no signal in oblivion.
lipstick? maybe.
if the world burns,
it can burn around a perfect red smile.

a text comes through:
*you up?*
it's him, of course.
the one who ghosted me in april,
because "commitment is a construct"
i consider replying -
something scathing, or sweet,
depending on how petty i feel
when the mushroom cloud arrives.

but then the kettle clicks off,
the sound almost tender.
i pour the water,

watch the steam curl like a question.
maybe the end of the world
isn't about endings at all -
just one last moment
to sit in your skin,
sip, swallow,
and choke back the universe.

**the note**

it was folded,
tucked between the pages
of a book i wasn't looking for,
its spine cracked,
the title faint as a half-forgotten dream.

the paper was thin,
creased with care,
edges softened by time,
like something carried too long in a pocket
or pressed into a drawer
among matches and stray buttons.

i opened it slowly,
as though it might break apart,
the ink faint but legible,
each letter curved with intention,
each word its own small breath.

*"to you—"*
it began,

a whisper on the page,
and already i was captured,
staring at a message meant
for someone i'll never meet.

the words ran on,
a stream of promises,
apologies,
memories sketched in black and white.
a place named,
a time remembered.
it wasn't meant for me,
but i read it like it was—
hungry for the story of these strangers,
for the life wrapped tight in these lines.

i held it close,
imagining them:
the hand that wrote it,
steady, or perhaps shaking,
the eyes that read it,
soft, or perhaps spilling over.

a lover's quarrel?
a farewell at a station?
the last gasp of something
too precious to lose?

the shop creaked around me,
rows of worn things
that no one wanted anymore,
each holding secrets
they could never tell.
and here i was,
a thief of ghosts,
stealing what little was left
of their story.

i slipped it back,
between the same pages,
in the same place.
the book went back on the shelf,
its weight heavier now.
i walked out into the cold,
thinking of the words,

the lives they carried,
the way some messages
never find their way home.

for the rest of the day,
it stayed with me,
that scrap of paper,
those fragile words,
a whisper in the back of my mind.
i never did buy the book.
but i wonder, still,
if someone else might,
if they'll find the note,
if they'll read it,
and wonder, too.

**mr grief**

grief's a bag for life you didn't choose -
the kind you find stuffed behind the door,
already torn, handles stretched to sinew,
smelling faintly of damp and something
sharp.

it follows you to the checkout queue,
where you fumble your change like loose
teeth.
you wear it to bed, an inside-out jumper,
its seams itching your skin,
its label scratching your neck.

grief sits at your table,
spreads crumbs in the butter dish,
drinks the last of the milk straight from
the carton.
it pulls faces in your window at night,
daring you to turn the light off.

some mornings, it shrinks,
slipping into a pocket like a crumpled receipt.
but by noon, it's back -
a shadow with elbows sharp as accusations,
banging into your ribs as you walk.

grief doesn't leave, it settles in,
tames the corners of its wild, sharp self.
one day, you'll catch it sleeping,
face slack, no teeth bared,
and you'll wonder why the silence feels so wrong.

**the bus ride**

it lumbers into view,
paint peeling like a bad habit.
we shuffle on, careful not to meet
the eyes of anyone we might know.
the driver's face: a marble carving,
indifferent as the ticket machine wheezes.

upstairs, the air is dense with yesterday's chips.
seats: a patchwork of stains and half-hearted graffiti,
the windows fogged with breath or time—
it's hard to tell which.

the cast arrives:
a man clutching a bag of tools like a newborn,
a woman whose perfume
climbs down your throat and won't let go,
teenagers in puffer jackets,

their shoes the colour of untied laces.

the bus jolts - every vertebra complains -
as we surge forward, a collective apology
for gravity itself.
someone moves for an elderly passenger,
awkward in their sudden saintliness,
while others remain sculptures,
immovable, resolute, part of the scenery.

we pass the usual sights:
a row of bins,
the house with the collapsed fence,
a pub that's changed its name
but not its clientele.
rain begins its slow rehearsal
against the windows,
turning the streets into muted ribbons.

behind me, a bag of sweets rattles.
each crunch a drumbeat,
breaking the spell of near-silence.

across the aisle, a man sleeps—
mouth agape, a hymn to surrender.

the engine groans as we near the stop.
people rise before the bus stills,
leaning into its final lurch like a shared instinct.
we scatter into the grey of the day,
carrying the smell of the journey with us—
grease, damp fabric,
and the faint ghost of tired dreams.

**my dead dog**

it starts with the leash,
coiled neatly by the door,
its snap still holding the shape
of your neck.

the bowl stays full longer now,
water rippling once a day
when i forget
and bump the edge with my foot.
the sound's unbearable,
like a question i don't want to answer.

on walks, my hands twitch
to hold something that isn't there.
the air feels emptier,
but the world keeps going,
oblivious to its loss.

sometimes i hear you:
the soft shuffle of paws in the hallway,

the weight of you shifting on the sofa.
i turn, hoping to catch
what i already know is gone.

i sweep the house for you in dreams -
under tables, behind curtains -
your tail a ghost
that wags just out of reach.

grief curls in the corner,
wearing your old shape.
i call it by your name.

**the date**

they sit at a table for two,
but it feels crowded -
him, her,
and the yawning gulf of mismatched ambition.

she stirs her drink like she's conjuring an escape plan,
each swirl a silent scream.
he's explaining crypto,
or his gym routine,
or some tragic combo of both,
his voice the sound of a fridge door left ajar.

her face is a study in hostage negotiation -
nodding, smiling, sipping at intervals
to stop herself from saying:
"this is my personal hell"

the waiter appears,
a saviour in black polyester.
"another drink?" he asks.
"yes" she answers too quickly,
her voice cracking like the thin veneer of
her patience.

he orders steak, rare,
and butchers the pronunciation of
"béarnaise"
she opts for the salad,
though her eyes linger on the wine list
like it's the only way out alive.

conversation dips into the murky depths
of his ex,
"crazy" he says, with a laugh that belongs
to a villain.
her hand clenches the napkin,
white knuckles glowing under dim lights.
somewhere deep inside, she begins
plotting his untimely demise.

dessert arrives -
a molten chocolate fondant that implodes
on impact.
she watches the mess ooze across the
plate,
and you can tell she's thinking:
that's my soul, right there.

when the bill comes, he makes a show
of reaching for his wallet,
only to pause,
"shall we split?"
and the waiter, god bless him,
stifles a laugh
because this man just tipped in coins.

they part at the door,
a handshake too formal,
his grin too smug.
she disappears into the night
like smoke from a car crash,

leaving him standing there,
confident he nailed it.

**old friend**

we stopped speaking,
not with a slam or a splinter,
but a quiet folding away of moments,
like clothes you forget to wear,
pushed deeper into the wardrobe.

i can't say what broke first.
maybe the air grew thinner,
the calls stretched longer,
until they snapped like tired elastic.
or maybe nothing broke -
it simply frayed, strand by strand,
until the knot between us loosened.

now, i hear your name
through someone else's mouth,
thin and pale,
a ghost of itself.
it lands like a knock at the door
i don't answer.

i remember the summers -
your laugh a stone skipping across water,
your face lit by the bonfire's molten
breath.
we were halves of the same thought,
one beginning where the other trailed off.

but memory's cruel.
it flattens the edges,
leaves out the parts where we got it wrong.
like the time we fought in the car -
your voice cracked;
i said something i shouldn't.
we never fixed it,
just moved forward
with the wound quietly bleeding.

i saw you once, years later,
at a café, hunched over a book,
your coffee cooling beside you.
i didn't call your name.
i told myself it wasn't the right time,

but the truth is,
i didn't know what to say.
what do you say to someone
who used to feel like a part of you
but now feels like a postcard
from somewhere you can't afford to visit?

i miss you.
not the you-now,
but the you-then.
and i miss the me who existed
when we fit,
before life turned us
into puzzles missing pieces.

if i called, would we speak
like strangers filling the silence
with small, polite words?
or would we crash together,
the way we used to,
like two waves that always knew
they were meant to meet?

i don't call.

but sometimes, i see your shadow

in my reflection -

a flicker,

a reminder

of what was,

and what might have been.

**the party hat**

woke up late again,
to the sound of nothing -
even the birds seemed bored.
put on the same hoodie
because it feels like a hug
from someone who doesn't mean it.

breakfast was a masterpiece:
stale toast, butter scraped
so thin you could see the bread's soul.
i laughed - actually laughed -
at the absurdity of it,
crumbs falling like a tiny tragedy
onto the floor i won't sweep.

the couch and i had another meeting.
we're practically married now,
its cushions fused to my body
like a lover who doesn't ask questions.
i flicked through channels,
landed on one of those nature shows.

the narrator said,
"some species abandon their weakest"
and i thought,
same.

by evening, it hit harder -
that quiet, sharp ache
like a missed step in the dark.
the tears showed up uninvited,
awkward guests at a party
where i'm the only one who showed.
i sat there, snotty and tragic,
thinking, *god, this is pathetic.*
and then i laughed so hard
it hurt.

it's funny, really,
how you can feel like nothing
and still feel *everything*.
how the sadness pulls up a chair,
but the absurdity is never far behind,
raising a glass in your honour,

cheeky grin, saying,
"cheers to this mess you call a life"

i put on a party hat -
why not?
wore it all evening,
even while brushing my teeth.
caught my reflection in the mirror,
and for a second,
i looked like someone
i might want to know.

**the picnic**

we planned it for weeks,
a family outing to prove
we're functional, happy,
and capable of sitting on grass
without starting a war.

the sun showed up like an unpaid intern,
half-hearted and late,
while the clouds loitered overhead,
muttering threats.
dad unfolded the tartan blanket,
which immediately absorbed
the damp earth's secrets.
mum unpacked sandwiches,
triangles of mediocrity,
the ham curling at the edges
like it already knew this was doomed.

the wasps arrived first,
militant and buzzing with glee.
"don't swat at them" mum warned,

as dad swatted.
cue chaos:
a drink spilled,
a scream,
uncle terry slapping himself
like he owed himself money.

then the wind picked up,
snatching napkins and dignity alike.
"hold the crisps" someone shouted,
but it was too late -
they spiralled into the sky,
golden flakes raining down
on unsuspecting hikers.

the football appeared next,
because apparently,
we hadn't suffered enough.
a single kick sent it straight
into the nearby lake,
where it bobbed,

a tragic reminder
of human hubris.

meanwhile, cousin jake
was attempting to start a fire -
"for ambience" he said,
as the flames licked dangerously close
to the plastic cutlery.
mum smacked him with a baguette.
the fire survived longer than his pride.

then came the rain,
a biblical downpour,
turning the field into a festival of mud.
dad slipped first,
his dignity following shortly after.
by the time we packed up,
we looked like a family
who'd crawled out of the trenches,
clutching soggy sausage rolls
like they were relics of a better time.

in the car, silence reigned,

except for the squelch of shoes

and the faint hum of resentment.

"well" mum said finally,

wringing out her hair.

"that was... fun"

and somehow,

we all laughed -

because what else can you do

when the picnic

turns into legend?

**passing shadows**

the house is still,
except for the rumble of the fridge
and the occasional creak of the
floorboards,
as if even they can feel the weight
of what's missing.

we pass each other
like shadows on opposite walls,
our words whittled down
to the practicalities of living:
milk, bin bags,
who's taking the car in for a service.

once, this kitchen was loud
with laughter and arguments
that meant something.
now, silence has moved in -
a third presence,
patient and smug.

the bed is colder,
though we still share it,
our bodies separated
by a void so vast
it feels like a different time zone.
your breathing is steady,
familiar,
but it doesn't soothe me anymore.

in the evenings, we sit
on opposite ends of the sofa,
bathed in the blue light of a screen,
pretending it's enough,
pretending we don't notice
how our knees never touch.

there's a pile of old photos
in the drawer by the tv.
i've stopped looking at them;
the smiles there feel
like strangers wearing our faces.
i wonder if you look at them

when i'm not home,
if you miss us
the way i do.

i used to know
the rhythm of your thoughts,
the shape of your dreams.
now, you're a closed book,
its spine uncracked,
its pages unwritten.
and i don't know
if it's me who stopped reading
or you who stopped speaking.

the clock ticks on,
indifferent.
the days pile up,
one after the other,
until they bury what we had.
and still,
we sit here,
side by side,

holding onto the bones of us,
as if they might grow flesh again.

**first day**

the boots sat by the door,
polished to a mirror shine,
reflecting nothing but the empty hall.
his coat hung loose on the peg,
its sleeves slack, as though even it
was too tired to hold him.

i made his tea the way he liked it,
two sugars, milk poured just after the bag.
he didn't finish it.
the spoon sat idle in the cup,
a faint ring left on the table -
a mark that would stay longer than him.

he stood in the doorway,
straight-backed,
his new uniform cutting him clean
from the boy i once knew,
the boy who ran barefoot in the garden,
laughing at the rain.

"don't forget your gloves"
i said, the words fragile,
too small to hold my fear.
he smiled, brief as a candle's flicker,
and picked them up,
his fingers brushing mine for a second
too brief to matter.

the door opened,
and the cold rushed in,
clinging to his shadow
as he stepped out.
the street swallowed him whole,
its silence louder than anything
i could bear.

i stayed by the window,
watching until his figure blurred
into the grey of the morning.
even then, i didn't move.
my hands stayed on the sill,
my breath on the glass,

as though holding my place
would keep him safe.

the kettle boiled again,
but i didn't pour.
the tea, like my words,
was no use now.

## made her mine

i met her where the rivers end in dust,
her hands were lanterns, her words a quiet fire.
she spoke in tongues the stars had long forgot,
each breath a thread, unspooling my desire.

but love is sand; it shifts beneath our fingers,
a dance of ghosts that haunt the open palm.
her scent still roams alone where evening lingers,
a rose crushed silent by a psalm.

she taught me how to hold the world and break it,
to drink from wounds and call it holy wine.

her eyes were temples; i burned as i forsake it,
the love that made me mortal, made her mine.

**meeting of minds**

we met like currents in a river,
two streams converging,
each carrying the weight of our worlds,
our histories etched in water.
you spoke of galaxies,
and i listened,
finding new stars between weird words.

your mind unfolded
like pages of a book i'd never read,
each thought a whisper of wonder,
each question an invitation.
i brought my own stories,
lines worn and creased,
and you showed me
where the light could shine through.

we grew in the spaces between -
in quiet pauses,
in the rhythm of shared breath.

you taught me to see the unseen,
to wonder at the edges of what i knew,
and i reminded you
of the beauty in the familiar.

our thoughts wove together,
a tapestry of learning and love,
each thread distinct yet inseparable.
we built bridges over doubts,
planted gardens in silences,
watched them bloom
with trust and time.

and now,
when our minds meet,
it's less collision
and more a handful of harmony -
a quiet song
only we can hear through laughter,
growing sweet
and sometimes sour
with every day that bids us

farewell.

**my tune**

i moved the chair myself this time,
the one you always pushed aside.
it scraped the floor with an awkward groan,
but it stood where i wanted it.

dinner for one is quiet now,
no salt-shakers dancing to your tune,
no napkins left crumpled like tiny flags
waving in surrender.

i've learned to fix the leaky tap,
its rhythmic drip no longer mocking.
i tightened the bolts, wiped my hands,
and filled the kettle for just one cup.

the silence isn't loud yet,
but it waits, coiled in the corners.
still, i carry on - laundry folded,
keys on the hook you never used.

sometimes, independence is a war,
a battle won in the tiny hours
when you thread a needle by yourself,
or laugh without looking for who hears.

i've planted flowers on the sill.
they bloom without your hand to water them.
and when the sun sets,
it sets only for me.

**mum and dad**

my parents speak in a secret language of
sighs.
dad's long and dramatic,
a shakespearean monologue in a single
breath,
mom's short and sharp,
punctuation marks on the silence.

they always ask if i'm eating enough,
as if my adulthood is some elaborate
famine.

dad keeps a drawer of cables for devices
no one's used since 1997,
saved as if one day the world will run on
vhs.

their thermostat wars could inspire
an epic novel.
the house becomes a sauna by dinner

and an ice rink by dessert.

they email me articles i've already read,
because the algorithm of parental instinct
always thinks it knows me better than i
know myself.

they tell stories out of sequence,
mixing decades like a playlist on shuffle.

they exist in a loop of endless routines,
but each repetition feels like a new
discovery.
every morning, they wonder if the coffee
tastes different.
every evening, they marvel at how dark it
gets this time of year.

and somehow, these little quirks
make everything feel more stable
than the ground beneath my feet.

**i hate you**

i hate the way you leave cups on the counter -
not in the sink, not in the dishwasher,
but perched like tiny porcelain anarchists,
taunting the universe with their defiance of order.

i hate how you fold laundry wrong on purpose,
shirts mangled into abstract origami tragedies,
as if picasso moonlights in our utility room.
you monster.

i hate your perfect hair that never cooperates
with gravity, wind, or my fragile sense of self-worth.
who wakes up looking like that?

are you sponsored by the gods? disgusting.

i hate how you finish my sentences,
usually with something smarter or
funnier.
let me flounder in my mediocrity in peace.
it's called self-expression, not a duet.

i hate how you remember obscure details,
like my favourite pen, which you bought in
bulk,
because apparently my joy is now your
side hustle.
i can't stand it.

and those inside jokes we share? i hate
them too,
the way they sneak up on me in meetings,
leaving me smirking like a lunatic
while everyone else discusses "quarterly
targets"

but most of all, i hate that i can't hate you properly.
believe me, i've tried.
i draft arguments in my head like legal briefs,
only to collapse into laughter when you walk in
with that stupid, perfect grin.

**nativity**

it wasn't the wise men this time,
just three lads from wigan
with a satnav and a boot full of lager.
bethlehem, wigan road,
not a star in sight,
just the dim glow of a costa.

mary's on maternity leave,
joseph's checking his fitbit -
27 steps pacing the ward -
and the baby?
well, he's crowning like a king
on double-time, christmas eve.

shepherds in high-vis jackets,
out on strike,
brought lamb vindaloo
wrapped in foil,
their gifts steaming
against the cold.

the angel, bless her,
got caught in the no-fly zone,
wing tips brushing
against easyjet.
'fear not' she said,
though no one was listening.

the inn's now a premier inn,
complete with vending machines.
no room, no manger,
but plenty of ice.
mary asks for prosecco;
joseph gets pepsi max.

out back, the cows
are mooing carols,
their breath steaming like tea.
the lads crack open
another tin of lager
and toast the boy:

'to the king of everything
and everyone else'
christmas on wigan road -
a holy night,
a proper one.

**stuffed**

the tree stands crooked, cheap tinsel clinging
like false hope to a year gone sideways.
mum's in the kitchen, battling pans
with the determination of someone
who's already lost.
"don't come in here!" she snaps -
as if we'd try.

dad's fiddling with the fairy lights again,
his hands all thumbs,
his muttering just loud enough
to make a point.
the box says twinkle mode,
but we're firmly set on flicker and fade.

nan's got her gin,
watching from the sofa like the ghost of christmas past.
"sprouts? you'll thank me for it later"

we won't.
the telly's droning some rerun
we all hate but endure,
a tradition, like disappointment.

the kids tear through paper and patience,
already bored of the plastic tat inside.
one whines about the batteries.
"ask your dad" mum says,
knowing full well he won't have any.
the cat sharpens its claws on a discarded box,
bored of us all.

dinner is served - a beige massacre.
the turkey, dry as an argument;
the stuffing, a mystery mum won't explain.
"just eat it" she says.
dad drowns his plate in gravy
and washes it down with silence.
uncle kev laughs too loud at his own jokes,

everyone else pretends not to hear.

by pudding, we're too full
to fake enthusiasm.
the flaming brandy catches -
almost too much -
but no one moves.
nan claps anyway,
because someone has to.

and when the evening settles,
we're all there,
picking at leftovers,
ignoring the cracks,
hoping next year
it'll all hold together better.

## the playground kings

they ruled the asphalt with scuffed trainers
and hair gelled into sharp, untouchable spikes,
their laughter the soundtrack to terror,
ricocheting off prefab walls,
painted the colour of dull mornings.

coats too big, collars popped like peacocks,
hands stuffed into pockets
deep as their imagined importance.
they circled the weak -
a pack of wolves on a diet of pasties
and boredom.

in pe, they swaggered,
shirts untucked,
calling us by names they'd invented,
names that stuck harder than glue
on the back of the school chairs.
behind the bike shed,

their cigarettes burned like badges,
orange embers in the drizzle.

the teachers didn't see,
or pretended not to -
their eyes fixed on registers,
detentions scribbled in faint biro.
"you lot, behave"
a mumble of authority
lost in the din of the lunch bell.

they didn't care.
they had the power of numbers,
of fists that knew the weight of silence,
of words that could unmake you
in front of a crowd
smirking into their polystyrene cups.

and yet, behind their bravado,
i'd catch it sometimes -
the crack.
a glance over the shoulder,
a hesitance before a punchline landed.

in the moment their jokes wavered,
you could almost see
the fear stitched under their skin,
as if they knew, deep down,
that the world would one day
shrink their shadows.

years later, in the queue at tesco,
one of them shuffled past me,
a grey uniform of his own:
hi-vis, work boots, a tired scowl.
our eyes met briefly.
no words.
the years had softened his edges,
but i still felt the weight of those days
like a bag of coins in my pocket.

i paid for my meal deal and left,
his laughter faint as a ghost
in the background jazz of the tills.

**seaside arcade**

the air tasted of vinegar and salt,
chips in greasy paper clutched like trophies.
a child cried over spilt ketchup -
a red streak on their jeans
that would never fully wash out.

the arcades glowed neon in the drizzle,
a siren's call of flashing lights and tinny music.
coins clinked into the machines,
fed like offerings into their hungry mouths.
a grabber claw dangled, hopeless,
fingers brushing stuffed bears
that never stood a chance.

mum hovered by the change machine,
her hand deep in her purse,
pulling out five-pound notes already damp
from too many pocket journeys.

dad leaned against the door,
a polystyrene cup steaming in his hand,
its coffee burnt, its purpose unclear.

inside, the kids darted from game to game
air hockey, followed by
the plastic guns of a zombie shooter,
clutched like they meant something.
every point won brought shrieks of triumph,
every loss a scowl that dissolved
into laughter seconds later.

the rain came heavier,
pigeons huddled under the eaves,
watching for dropped chips
or a wayward doughnut.

lunch was eaten in the car,
legs pressed awkwardly against the seatbacks.
fish and chips, lukewarm now,

peeling batter and chips limp from the paper.
someone had splurged on a stick of rock,
already sticky,
its minty stripes jagged and unwrapped.

the 2p machines claimed the last of the change,
cascading coins over the metal edges,
while mum sighed,
calculating what could have been spent elsewhere.
outside, the rain hit harder,
the grey sky folded into itself,
but no one wanted to leave yet.

when the power cut came,
a brief gasp of darkness,
the arcades fell silent -
just the sound of the sea roaring
somewhere far off,
a reminder that none of this,

not the lights or the games or the chips,
could ever drown it out.

**flesh sanctuary**

you don't need the building,
the stone, the glass,
the bells that call
like hands cupped around a prayer.

you don't need to kneel on cold wood,
the grain pressing into your skin
as though to mark you holy.

instead, light the candle of yourself:
hold the flame steady
against the winds of indifference.
let your breath be the hymn,
your touch the sacrament,
your kindness the psalm
sung without words.

be the open door,
the space where someone's silence
can stretch out,

unfolding itself
like an old coat.

the world turns anyway,
sky cathedraled by trees,
clouds tracing windows in the blue.
every river whispers
its own amen.

you don't need the walls -
only the hands
to lift someone when they fall.

**the plan**

it was all set -
a grand exit,
dramatic, poignant,
the kind of thing that would make
a stranger in the street
shed a tear without knowing why.

i'd written the note:
brief, clever,
just enough edge to haunt them.
not too much -
you don't want to seem needy.

everything was ready,
then the cat walked in,
eyes like twin accusations,
tail flicking in disapproval.
'who'll open the tins?' he seemed to say.
'who'll clean the litter box?'
the absurdity of it almost killed me first.

then mum called,
asking if i'd remembered
to pick up her prescription.
"useless" she said,
half-laughing, half-right.
and suddenly, i pictured her,
still nagging
even if i wasn't there to hear it.

i sat there, stuck -
between the weight of it all
and the sheer stupidity of my timing.
the toaster popped,
like punctuation,
and i thought:
might as well eat first.

the day stretched out,
each hour taunting me
with its ordinary demands.
emails piled up;
the sink filled with dishes.

and somewhere between
scrubbing forks
and deleting spam,
the chores caught me off guard.

if life was a cruel joke,
it was one i wasn't ready
to stop laughing at.
so i sat back down,
the cat now purring in my lap,
and thought:

*not today.*
maybe tomorrow,
but first -
there's milk to buy,
bins to take out,
and a prescription to pick up.

## encounter in aisle five

it happens near the tinned tomatoes,
as if my heart isn't enough of a pulp
already.
there you are, angled just so,
reading the label on something red -
your shoulders still too sure of themselves,
your hair untamed in that way
that used to feel like mine to fix.

my first instinct is to escape -
to drop the basket, fake a cough,
dive into the safety of frozen peas.
but it's too late.
you look up,
and there's that flicker,
half-recognition, half hesitation,
like we're both waiting
for the punchline of a joke
neither of us told.

your smile arrives late,
like a train delayed by years.
i return it,
awkwardly,
the kind of smile
that feels like wearing someone else's shoes.
we close the gap,
me clutching spaghetti hoops
like they'll shield me.

"hi" you say,
and it's not much,
but the sound of your voice
untucks the corners of old memories.
i nod,
as if nodding could fold them back.

you ask how i've been,
your head tilting slightly,
just enough for me to see
you don't actually care,

and neither do i.
still, we do the dance:
fine, busy, working a lot -
the universal song of people
pretending not to hurt.

you mention someone,
a name that lands too softly
for me to know its shape.
your hands gesture,
filling in blanks
i don't want to picture.
i murmur something,
words slippery in my mouth,
and grip the basket tighter.

we linger,
caught between aisles
of what we were
and what we'll never be again.
the fluorescent lights wink above us,
unforgiving,

casting shadows on truths
we don't dare unpack.

and then it's over.
you glance at your watch,
a signal,
a lifeline to pull yourself away.
"good to see you"
you say,
and for a moment,
i believe you mean it.

i watch you walk off,
your footsteps soft on the linoleum.
for a second,
i almost follow,
but then the tin in my hand reminds me:
spaghetti hoops are enough
for tonight.

i move to the next aisle,
pretending not to notice

the taste of something sharp

lingering on my tongue.

**in translation**

it starts with a smile,
wide, desperate,
the kind you'd give
a teacher you hope won't call on you.
the man behind the counter nods,
waiting for words
i can't quite summon.

i point at the menu,
but my finger lands
between two dishes.
he raises an eyebrow -
a question, an invitation -
and i nod, as if that clears anything up.

in the market,
a woman with a loud scarf
hands me fruit i didn't ask for,
her words rolling toward me,
melodic and baffling.

i nod again.
it's become my universal reply.

the taxi driver laughs,
a low, rumbling sound,
when i butcher his city's name.
what i say means nothing,
but he drives anyway,
the road bending under us
like it knows the way better than i do.

at dinner,
the waiter gestures to a plate
of something unfamiliar,
something glistening and alive with sauce.
i eat it, smile,
and murmur what i hope is thank you.
he laughs, correcting me gently.
what i said translates to
"i admire your mother"

it becomes a dance -
me fumbling with phrases

torn from a guidebook,
them gracious, amused,
their kindness stretching across syllables.
i string words together
like mismatched beads,
hoping they don't notice
the gaps between them.

in the end, it's the gestures that matter:
a hand over my heart,
a raised glass,
a shrug paired with a grin.
we build a language of our own,
clumsy but effective,
a patchwork of attempts and good
intentions.

and when i leave,
the man at the counter waves,
the woman in the market nods,
the taxi driver gives me
a thumbs-up that feels like a medal.

i'll take it -

victory in the smallest of wars,

proof that sometimes,

even the wrong words

can take you exactly where you need to go.

**the umbrella**

it happened at the crossing -
rain stitching the air
into grey curtains,
the kind that soak you before you notice.

i stood there,
coat failing,
hands stuffed into pockets
as though they could warm themselves.
the light turned green,
and still, i lingered,
watching puddles ripple
with the weight of passing cars.

then you appeared,
a figure in a dark coat,
your face half-hidden beneath an
umbrella,
its black dome sheltering you
from the world's wetness.
you stopped beside me,

close enough that i felt
the dry pocket of air
you carried.

without a word,
you shifted, tilted the umbrella
so its edge caught my shoulder.
i turned, startled,
ready to explain or apologize,
but you smiled,
quick, easy,
like this was nothing.

we crossed together,
two strangers sharing
the same small roof,
our feet splashing in tandem.
the rain hissed around us,
a quiet protest against your kindness.

at the far curb,
you nodded,
folded the umbrella shut,

and disappeared into the blur
of weather and crowds,
leaving me there,
half-dry,
half-something i couldn't name.

it wasn't much -
a tilt of fabric,
a moment of grace -
but it stayed with me,
long after the rain had stopped.

**the ghost of home**

i stepped off the train,
bag heavy on my shoulder,
shoes still carrying the dust of elsewhere.
the air smelled the same,
or close enough:
wet concrete, diesel fumes,
the faintest trace of something green.
but it caught in my throat differently now,
sharper, thinner,
like an old song played in the wrong key.

the high street stretched out ahead,
still patched with cracked pavement,
the same shops clustered like gossipers.
but the bakery was gone,
its windows darkened,
and the corner pub stood quieter,
as if the bricks themselves
had grown tired of holding the past.

i walked the long way,
through streets that once knew
the slap of my trainers,
my breath quick from racing shadows.
the park still lingered where i'd left it,
its grass sparser,
its swings rusting into memory.
i stopped to sit,
but the bench creaked beneath me,
and i rose again,
as though it no longer wanted my weight.

the house came into view suddenly,
as though it had leapt from hiding.
the paint was new,
bright and brash,
the windows glaring back at me -
strangers now,
unfamiliar eyes in a familiar face.
the hedge i once squeezed through
was trimmed to perfection,

its wildness tamed,
its secret passages erased.

i lingered on the pavement,
fingers brushing the strap of my bag,
as if touching something real
might anchor me.
the curtains twitched,
and for a moment,
i thought i saw her -
the shape of mum,
hurrying to the window
to see if it was me.
but the face was wrong,
the outline sharper,
the weight of a stranger's life
filling the space where ours once lived.

i turned,
walking back toward the station,
passing old haunts that no longer called
my name.

the chip shop had changed hands;
the playground had lost its charm.
the streets seemed narrower now,
the sky lower,
and i wondered if it was me
or the years
that had stolen their magic.

on the train back,
i stared at my reflection in the window,
fuzzy, doubled,
split between what was
and what i'd become.
home, i realized,
isn't in the bricks,
or the streets,
or the swings that still creak in the wind.

it's the weight of a laugh
caught in the walls,
the smell of toast at midnight,
the way the floor remembers your step.

it's the story a place tells
when you still belong to it.

and though this place
once wore my name,
its pages had turned,
its tale rewritten,
and i was just a stranger
passing through a life
i no longer knew how to live.

**the first sip**

it hits the tongue like revelation,
like the universe condensed into one cool,
glorious drop.
you'd think i'd never tasted water before,
like it's the nectar of gods
and not the same tap dribble
i've ignored all day.

my throat opens – hallelujah -
a hymn sung silently
to the holy grail of hydration.
each gulp feels profound,
like it's curing something ancient,
something primal,
the ghost of every dry spell
i've ever endured.

it's not graceful.
i guzzle like a child let loose at a party,
liquid spilling from the corners of my mouth,

trickling down my chin
like i'm auditioning for a survival
documentary.

halfway through, i pause -
an act of self-restraint
worthy of a medal -
and look at the glass,
now half-empty (or half-full,
but let's not get philosophical).

i swear it glows,
shimmering in the kitchen light
like a trophy.
it's just water, i tell myself.
plain. ordinary.
then take another sip -
and wonder why i ever doubted.

**before the party**

the house holds its breath,
each room a quiet conspiracy.
chairs sit stiff-backed,
their arms folded,
waiting for the weight of strangers.
the table stretches out,
bare and expectant,
its surface gleaming like a polished lie.

the air is thick with waiting,
a kind of pause that aches.
curtains twitch slightly,
brushed by a breeze
that seems to know
what's coming.

in the kitchen,
wine bottles huddle together,
labels straightened,
caps unscrewed but not yet poured.
the fridge hums to itself,

a nervous undertone
in the silence.

you wander through it all -
a ghost of intent,
checking glasses,
straightening cushions,
turning every light just so.
your breath is louder than it should be,
your hands too eager
to fidget with nothing.

outside, the garden waits,
its grass damp with dusk,
candles unlit,
each one a promise
still sleeping in its jar.

and then, the clock ticks louder.
the doorbell rings once,
like a spark in the dark.
the house shifts its weight,
shakes off its stillness.

the night begins,
its quiet undone
in the tumble of voices,
the clash of plates,
the music lifting the silence
to its feet.

**the man in the mirror**

it hit me in the bathroom,
like these things always do,
mid-shave, razor paused
as i stared at the face
i barely recognised anymore.
the skin hung different -
looser, somehow tired -
and there, lurking near my temple,
a single grey hair,
mocking me under the bathroom light.

this is what they don't warn you about:
you're still *you*,
but less polished,
like a sofa sagging where people once sat.
i've become a man
who moisturises after 30,
uses words like "self-care"
and buys shoes for their comfort.

once, i was the kind of idiot
who drank tequila straight
and called it personality.
now, i measure caffeine after noon
like a scientist avoiding disaster.
my knees creak when i stand -
a private symphony -
and somewhere along the way,
i became the guy who says,
"can't beat a good night in."

i used to care about rebellion,
burning bright, being dangerous,
but last week,
i caught myself tutting
at someone parking badly.
i own a spice rack.
i alphabetised it.
there's balsamic vinegar in my cupboard
and i know what it's for.

the music of my youth,
once a holy grail of noise,
now sounds suspiciously like chaos.
i listen to podcasts about history
on purpose.
the volume of my ambitions
has dulled, too,
no longer a roar,
but a whistle i barely notice
between meals.

i've stopped fighting the inevitable:
tupperware lids that don't match,
a wardrobe that knows no trends,
the slow creep of routines
where spontaneity used to be.
but there are flashes,
moments when i see him -
the boy i was -
peering through these tired eyes.

he's laughing at me, of course.
at my annual health checks,
my stretch marks,
my habit of googling symptoms
at midnight.
and i laugh back,
because what he doesn't know yet
is that this version of me -
this weary, ridiculous,
mortgaged version -
is somehow still standing.

so i shave,
rinse the razor,
pat the face i've grown into.
the man in the mirror stares back,
grey hair and all,
and i nod to him,
because we've made it this far,
and that's no small thing.

**the woman in the mirror**

it crept up slowly,
like rain seeping through a cracked
window.
i didn't notice at first -
the lines gathering around my eyes,
soft whispers of years passed,
the kind that no cream can erase.
and now here i am,
in this bathroom lit too harshly,
facing the woman
who looks like she's borrowed my face
and forgotten to give it back.

the hair's not mine,
not really -
streaks of silver threading through brown
like someone else's design.
i pluck one,
a futile ritual,
because for every one i pull,

another waits in the wings.
but i pull it anyway,
because some habits refuse to die.

i lean closer,
inspect the freckles
that were once delicate,
now sprawled across my cheeks
like they've given up behaving.
i trace a scar on my chin -
a memory from some time ago,
too faint to recall,
but not faint enough to forget.

the cupboard under the sink
is a graveyard of promises:
serums, creams,
a facemask that cost too much
and delivered nothing.
i know this,
but i keep buying them,
hoping for miracles in jars.

i remember when this face
was something i weaponised,
a thing that turned heads,
stopped conversations.
now it's quieter,
a little softer,
like a song smirking under your breath.
and it's fine, really,
most of the time.

but some days,
i catch her -
the girl i was -
in the corner of my reflection.
she's laughing at me,
mocking my sensible shoes,
my bedtime routine,
the way i now find joy
in herb gardens and clean countertops.

she doesn't know yet
how much she'll grow to love

the quiet victories:
the way the world slows
when you let it,
how wine tastes better
when you drink it slowly,
how a night in,
wrapped in the smell of lavender oil,
can feel like salvation.

i pull back,
look at the whole picture.
this woman isn't her -
isn't the girl
who thought forever
was something she'd already earned.
but she's here,
holding the gaze,
smiling faintly.

i wash my hands,
smooth the lines on my blouse,
and step back into the day.

the woman in the mirror stays behind,
watching me go,
proud in her own quiet way.

**unseen**

the street is alive,
a tide of faces sweeping past,
each one carved from their own urgency.
feet strike the pavement in mismatched rhythms,
a chorus of lives i'll never know.
i walk among them,
a thread lost in the weave,
unpulled, unnoticed.

the man with the briefcase strides ahead,
his phone pressed tight to his ear,
his words swallowed by engines and brakes.
the woman to my left adjusts her scarf,
lips moving in silent rehearsal,
her world turning just out of reach.

i pass a café,
its windows lit with a golden glow.
laughter spills through the cracks,

but it isn't mine.
behind the glass, they lean forward,
hands wrapped around cups,
their joy sharp and contained.

the sky shifts,
its grey edges blurring into darker shades,
and still, the crowd moves -
each step, a decision,
each glance, a deflection.
no one sees me,
not really.
i'm part of the scenery,
a coat in motion,
a shadow without a source.

at the crossing,
i wait with them,
our bodies pressed close
but our lives held apart.
a child tugs on their mother's hand,
the gesture so small,

it aches.
a man whistles softly to himself,
his tune dissolving into the wind.

when the light turns green,
we surge forward,
a wave breaking against the curb.
my steps blend into theirs,
each one indistinct,
each one dissolving into the next.

by the time i reach the far side,
i've forgotten my own weight,
lost in the pull of this city's heart.
but somewhere,
deep in the swell of the crowd,
i feel it -
a flicker, a knot of something real,
even if no one else does.

**the room you left behind**

it began with the curtains.
they hung limp, too heavy with dust,
their fabric trapping the light
like something unspoken.
the air here felt damp with silence,
a kind of stillness
that only lingers where people used to be.

your shoes sat by the door,
laces undone,
mud crusted in the cracks of the soles.
i almost tripped over them,
as if you'd left them there
to remind me of something
i wasn't ready to know.

the dresser was next.
its drawers groaned as they opened,
revealing a world i hadn't prepared for:
pressed shirts folded with military
precision,

coins scattered like crumbs
in the velvet of a jewellery box.
and there, at the bottom,
a notebook, spine cracked,
its pages filled with your half-written
thoughts.
i read them, one by one,
your words tracing paths
i could never follow.

the kitchen table was stacked with papers,
their corners curling like old leaves.
lists, receipts,
a note in your handwriting:
"meet at 3. don't forget."
i tried to guess who you'd meet,
but the name wasn't there.

on the bookshelf,
your favourite mug sat upside down,
its rim chipped from mornings
you never talked about.

next to it, a jar of pennies,
each one tarnished,
like the life you'd been saving for
but never quite spent.

the wardrobe whispered secrets
in moth-eaten sleeves:
a jacket i never saw you wear,
a scarf i didn't know you owned.
there was a pocket knife, too,
its blade dull with age,
and a photograph tucked into its sheath -
a place by the sea,
but no faces,
only waves crashing into rocks
that refused to move.

and then, in the farthest corner,
a box i almost missed.
inside:
a letter sealed but unsent,
addressed to no one i knew.

your handwriting wavered,
like you weren't sure you meant it.
i didn't open it -
not yet.

i left the room,
closing the door behind me,
but not all the way.
the things you left behind
were still here,
still heavy,
still holding the shape of you
in their quiet refusal to let go.

**close call**

it wasn't heroic -
no hollywood dive,
no slow-motion gasp.
just me, shuffling across the street,
hands stuffed in my coat
against the wind that had decided
i deserved to suffer.

the car came out of nowhere -
or maybe i wasn't looking.
either way, it skidded to a halt,
a symphony of screech and smoke,
as i stood there,
mid-step,
with all the grace of a startled goat.

the driver rolled down his window—
his face pink with rage,
or relief,
or whatever colour
nearly killing someone makes you.

"you alright, mate?"
like i might say no,
collapse in a heap,
and ruin his afternoon.

i waved him on,
because what else do you do
when your life flashes before your eyes
and all it shows
is a loop of you eating crisps
on the sofa?

the pedestrians stared,
as if they'd witnessed a miracle.
one woman clutched her shopping bag
like it was rosary beads,
while a kid laughed,
pointing at my wet wobble
as if it was the best thing
he'd seen all week.

the car moved on,
its engine grumbling,

and i crossed the road,
suddenly aware
of how ridiculous i looked.
legs like jelly,
heart pounding louder
than my excuses.

i didn't die.
but for the rest of the day,
every step felt like a risk -
stairs leered,
pavements narrowed,
even pigeons gave me
a sidelong glance,
as if to say,
"careful, mate. one of us
might finish the job"

later, i sat at home,
staring at my tea,
half-convinced the kettle
was plotting against me.

and all i could think was this:
i survived -
not because i was lucky,
but because i'm not important enough
for the universe
to bother killing yet.

**lost hour**

i was supposed to be somewhere.
not here,
perched on a damp bench,
watching the sky stretch itself thin
over a field that doesn't even belong to me.

the trees swayed in slow-motion
arrogance,
their branches flexing like they'd been
designed by god himself.
and the sun -
don't get me started on the sun -
draped itself all over the place,
turning the horizon into molten gold
just to show off.

i should have checked my phone,
the small rectangle of guilt
buzzing faintly in my pocket.
but no, i was transfixed -
a moth to nature's gaudy lightbulb,

all wide-eyed wonder
and absolutely no sense of priorities.

the minutes stacked up like bad decisions.
the clouds shifted,
turning bruised and dramatic,
as if they knew
they were the main event.
a single bird cut through the sky,
its wings slicing the air
like it had somewhere to be.
not like me,
who clearly didn't.

when i finally checked the time,
it hit like a slap -
an hour gone, vanished,
the kind of theft you can't report.
i was late,
of course,
and for nothing heroic:

just staring at leaves,
at a horizon that wouldn't remember me.

later, when i apologised,
i couldn't say why.
you can't explain
to someone waiting at a cold bus stop
that you got caught up
watching light bounce off water
like a cheap magic trick.

and yet, for all the lateness,
all the guilt -
i'd do it again.
sit there,
while the world painted itself over me,
its colours too bright to ignore,
its time too slippery to hold.

**the noise**

it started small,
a creak,
like the floorboards testing their voice.
i told myself it was the house,
settling its old bones,
a thing houses do -
don't they?

but then came the second sound,
a shuffle, deliberate,
just beyond the reach of the hallway light.
i froze, halfway to the fridge,
milkless, breath tight,
as if not moving
would make me less edible.

the dark loomed around the corner,
thicker than usual,
like it had taken up a gym membership
just to mess with me.
another shuffle - closer this time -

and i clutched the nearest weapon:
a spatula,
because apparently,
i was ready to sauté my attacker.

logic began its slow retreat.
"just the wind-" it whispered,
though the windows were shut tight.
"or the neighbour's cat" it tried,
but no cat i'd ever met
walked with footsteps
heavy as regret.

the fridge hummed -
unhelpfully.
i stared at the door,
now a portal to nowhere i wanted to go.
this was it, i thought.
the headline wrote itself:
"local idiot found spatula-clutching in nightwear"

i took a step forward,
the kind of step
that makes knees rethink their purpose.
the shadows seemed to lean in,
greedy,
and i wondered if they'd always been so sharp.

and then i saw it -
a shape, hunched,
indistinct yet too distinct.
it moved,
or maybe the light shifted,
but it was enough
to make my heart launch
into an ill-advised sprint.

i lunged,
spatula first,
a hero in mismatched socks,
only to strike something solid.
the shape fell with a thud,

and there it was -
the thing that haunted my night.

a laundry basket.
full of my own socks,
sitting smug on the floor,
having staged the performance of its life.

i stood there, shaking,
feeling both alive and entirely ridiculous.
the dark laughed silently,
its joke complete.
and the fridge,
traitorous,
just kept on humming.

**the old couple**

it wasn't the way they moved,
slow and steady,
as though time itself had softened its grip.
it was the hands -
hers resting in his,
the fingers curled like ivy,
a quiet claiming of what was already
theirs.

they passed the café,
where steam pressed itself
to the glass,
their faces slipping out of focus
with each step forward.
she wore a coat too big for her frame,
its hem brushing the ground,
while his hat sat slightly askew,
like he'd forgotten where it belonged.

i watched from the bench,
pretending not to stare,

pretending their touch didn't pull me
into their gravity.
his arm twitched,
just enough to shift her closer.
she laughed -
a sound too soft to carry far
but loud enough
to fill the street.

at the crossing,
he glanced both ways,
his grip firm on hers,
a small, practised gesture
that said everything
without saying it.
and when the light changed,
they moved together,
one foot, then the other,
their shadows stitching themselves
into the cracks of the pavement.

what stories did they hold
beneath their skin?
what arguments,
what whispered apologies,
what promises made in the dark
still vibrated between their ribs?

they disappeared into the afternoon,
their silhouettes shrinking,
but not gone.
i stayed there a little longer,
as if waiting for something
i hadn't known i'd lost.

## the midnight olympics

it starts with a twist,
the sheets curling around my legs
like clingfilm,
the pillow sulks beneath my head,
flattened by its failure
to deliver peace.

i check the clock—
1:47.
a time that feels invented,
too late to matter,
too early to exist.
the house is a tomb,
except for the fridge,
its low drone the anthem of my failure.

i try counting sheep,
but they're uncooperative—
leaping fences with the enthusiasm
of understudies who know
they'll never make the lead.

their hooves clatter,
mocking me with each bound.

i shift, roll,
try the other side of the bed -
the side apparently cursed
to make my spine regret everything.
the duvet slides off
and lands in a heap,
taunting me from the floor
like a lover mid-argument.

outside, the streetlight flickers,
a stuttering companion
to my misery.
i hear a fox screech -
its call sharp and reckless,
as if it too
has given up on sleep.

by 3:00,
my thoughts turn feral:
what if i never sleep again?

what if i become one of those people
with bloodshot eyes and strange hobbies,
like restoring vintage toasters
or memorising train timetables?

i try breathing exercises,
counting to ten,
but by seven i'm wondering
why i said that thing
to jessica in 2016.
did she ever forgive me?
does she even remember?

at 4:22,
i surrender.
the kitchen greets me with cold tiles,
the kettle boils with the arrogance
of someone who's never known
exhaustion.
i sit in the dark,
cup in hand,

watching the clock tick toward morning
like it's racing me to nowhere.

by dawn,
i'm a shell -
but at least i've solved the big questions:
where the missing sock went,
why the moon looks so tired,
and exactly how long
a night can stretch.

**a first encounter**

she knelt where the grass grew patchy,
the earth beneath her knees soft and
damp,
her hand hovering, hesitant,
as though the thing before her
held the weight of the world.

a worm, pale as moonlight,
curled itself from the soil,
its body a ribbon of quiet persistence.
she gasped, not with fear,
but with the wonder
that only comes
when everything is new.

her fingers, small and unsure,
reached out like a question.
she touched it lightly,
then recoiled, laughing -
a sound like the first drop of rain
on an open field.

"why does it move like that?"
she asked,
but not to me.
the worm twisted,
a silent reply
that she alone could understand.

the sunlight poured through the trees,
stitching shadows across her back.
she leaned in closer,
her curiosity bold,
her wonder unbroken.
and i watched,
quietly,
from the edge of her world,
where time hung suspended
on the thread of her discovery.

what was it like to feel so alive?
to press your hands into the dirt
and find a secret
waiting to be named?

to see the ordinary
for the first time,
as if it had been placed there
just for you?

she looked up,
her face full of the moment,
and i thought to tell her
about the world,
about all the wonders
that would fade too quickly,
or the burdens
she'd yet to carry.

but instead,
i said nothing,
letting her hold her joy
a little longer.
the worm burrowed back into the earth,
and she watched it go,
her eyes following
until there was nothing left to see.

**the edge of knowing**

the air thickens in the quiet,
each second a pebble dropped
into a bottomless well.
the ceiling light flickers -
just once -
and it feels like a bad omen.

i sit by the window,
watching the sky inch darker,
clouds pulling across it
like someone drawing a curtain too slowly.
outside, the leaves barely stir,
frozen in their own suspense.
even the birds seem to wait,
perched and watchful,
their wings folded tight.

the table is cluttered -
a mug half-full of cold tea,
a pen rolled into the corner.
i pick it up,

then put it down,

then pick it up again,

like its weight could ground me.

the silence grows louder,

a pressure building in the room.

i tap my foot

against the chair leg,

the rhythm uneven,

a heartbeat trying to steady itself.

in the distance,

a car engine grumbles,

then fades.

a dog barks once,

sharp,

and the echo cuts through me

like a question i don't want to answer.

i think of opening a book,

but the words would scatter,

unread.

i think of turning on the radio,

but every song would feel
too bright, too wrong.

instead, i wait,
hands clasped tightly,
palms damp with the sweat of waiting.
each breath is deliberate,
dragged in and pushed out,
as if i have to remind myself
how to stay present.

when the sound comes -
a knock, a buzz, a voice -
it feels distant,
like i'm hearing it through water.
i stand,
slowly,
as if moving too quickly
might shatter the moment.

i reach the door, the phone,
the answer,
and for a moment,

time holds itself still,
suspended on the edge
of what might be.

i don't open it yet.
not quite.
the weight of the unknown
is heavy,
but for now,
i can still carry it.

## the inkless author

i am the whisper between pages,
the ink that runs too thin,
a nameless signature stamped on a
thought,
yours, but never begun in you.
i am the shifting shadow
of voices borrowed, returned,
a crowd in one room,
crowded still by absence.

each word is a mirror,
pressed to your face,
and in its reflection,
i vanish, dissolve,
the shape of a silence
you did not notice speaking.

call me the architect of ghosts,
or the hand that builds
with bricks of breath,
no walls, no roof, only thresholds.

i am the author who is authored,
a question written in the ink of answers
i will never own.

to be everyone and no one,
to wear your thoughts like borrowed coats,
to vanish into what is seen.
do you feel me there,
a crease in your certainty,
a pause too long to ignore?

my sentences are strangers to me.
i birth them and lose them,
a mother watching her children
climb over the edge of knowing.
they return with stories of places
i will never walk,
of faces i have forgotten wearing.

i am not here, but you are.
i am not you, but i am.
the words know no allegiance,
they are smoke,

and i am their match,
struck and spent,
leaving nothing but ash,
the scent of becoming.

**what is love?**

love is the smell of burnt toast at 3 a.m.,
the silence after an argument loud enough
to break light bulbs and promises,
a bouquet of supermarket flowers
wilting in the passenger seat
as you rehearse an apology
that never sounds good aloud.

it's splitting the last chip and
resenting how much ketchup they take.
it's the sweaty duvet of forgiveness,
thrown over your head like a hostage hood,
and the sour breath of compromise
whispering "stay" into the damp of your pillow.

love is laughing at their jokes
when the punchline is always you.
it's scrolling through their ex's instagram
and pretending it's research.

it's counting the seconds they're late
and counting the seconds they leave early.

love is the golden retriever grin of hope,
wagging its tail at the locked door.
it's the poetry we recite
when the meter's broken
and every rhyme is cheap.

love is the world's longest joke—
you laugh until your ribs ache,
until the punchline
is a tear
you swear is just dust
in your eye.

## alternative lives

the clock ticks like a disappointed parent.
i sit in the plush beige purgatory
of "we'll call you shortly"
imagining the lives i left behind.

what if i'd married that boy from leeds,
the one with a tattoo of garfield
and a dream of starting a food truck?
we'd be serving lasagna from a van by now,
our kids named after condiments.

or if i'd stuck with my teenage ambition—
professional ghostwriter for reality stars.
"chapter 3: my gym tan laundry journey"
a bestseller i'd never dare admit was mine.

i could've been a beekeeper in brighton,
queen of the hives,
a little smug about saving the planet,
but smug in a sustainable way.

or a librarian. quiet, respected,
in charge of overdue books and secret
lives.

instead, here i am,
polishing a cv like a dubious trophy,
"excellent communication skills"
burning holes in my soul,
while the receptionist calls
the guy after me.

i straighten my tie,
adjust my hopeful smile.
this is the life i chose.
or maybe, it chose me.
i'll save the bees later.

**the babysitter**

we should have known by the boots:
steel-toed, scratched like a feral cat's cv.
she arrived with a cigarette dangling
from the corner of her mouth,
lit by the time she crossed the threshold.

"kids, eh?" she muttered,
spitting her gum into a potted plant.
"which one's the least annoying?"

she didn't so much sit the kids
as glare them into submission.
toby's bedtime story was *the art of war,*
read aloud in a voice like an ashtray.
mia asked for a glass of water -
was handed a mug of black coffee.
"no cream" the babysitter said,
"builds character"

by 9 p.m, she'd rearranged the furniture,
turning the living room into a dojo.

"discipline starts at home," she barked,
as the children practiced planking
while she sipped from a flask labelled
"medicine"

when toby tried to escape,
she caught him with a look so sharp
it sliced through his dreams of freedom.
"i once babysat a goat" she said,
"and it had better manners than you"

by 10, the kids were in bed,
whispering prayers to the gods of childcare.
the babysitter turned to us,
parents back too early.
"fifty quid," she said,
"and you're lucky i didn't charge for therapy"

we paid in silence,
watched her swagger into the night.
the kids don't ask for babysitters

anymore.

toby calls her *sensei.*

mia keeps a tin of coffee under her bed,
just in case.

**her, mate**

she's a walking riddle, yeah?
not the clever kind, though—more like,
"why are your shoes in the fridge again?"
hair like a storm nobody warned you
about,
a fringe so crooked it might be morse code
for *help me.*

she's got this laugh, mate,
like a car alarm meeting its end,
and teeth that could outshine
a streetlamp - on a foggy day, maybe.
she smells like coconut shampoo
and mild regret.

personality? top notch.
she calls me *champion* when i screw up
and *plankton* when i'm right.
hates cats, loves stray pigeons.
once gave a fiver to a bloke

playing a kazoo outside tesco,
said he was "misunderstood."

she's clever in that way that's dangerous,
quotes nietzsche while burning toast.
told me the world's a simulation
as she tripped over her own feet
and blamed *the patriarchy.*

when she talks about fixing
the ozone layer
or how dolphins are just *too smug,*
you think, *yeah, that's the one.*

and if she ever leaves?
i'll miss the chaos, mate,
the way she makes the ordinary seem
like a really dodgy heist movie.
but until then, i'll keep wondering
why there's coconut shampoo in my fridge.

**hands**

you don't think about them, do you?
not until they betray you -
a tremor holding the cup,
the crack of knuckles like splintering ice.

but they remember.
the first time they gripped a pencil,
drew a house with no roof
and called it home.
the first time they touched another's face
and didn't pull back.

they've known work:
turning screws that wouldn't budge,
scrubbing floors until water went grey,
pulling weeds that always grew back.
they've held grief,
in the way they couldn't hold it at all.

but there's joy, too,
in their quiet rebellion -

the way they fold around an apple,
slice bread without thinking,
cup light through a crack in the curtains.

they've built your life,
piece by piece,
fingerprints stamped on everything
you'll never quite get right.

one day, they'll forget you,
curl into themselves,
a closing fist of memory.
but for now,
they're yours.
use them.

**the package**

it arrived on a thursday,
the kind of day
that smells of reheated soup
and indifference.
no return address, no stamp -
just my name, scrawled
in handwriting that leaned too hard
into itself, like it knew secrets
and wouldn't tell.

the postman shrugged.
"not my problem" he muttered,
his eyes on the door
like it might swallow him whole.

i brought it in,
the box lighter than it should've been,
like whatever it held
had ideas of leaving.
the cat hissed.
the dog whimpered.

even the fridge clicked,
its cold heart refusing to care.

i didn't open it straight away -
there's a ritual to these things.
i made tea,
washed the same mug twice.
googled *mysterious packages and what they mean,*
found nothing useful,
just forums full of people
who'd never received one.

it sat on the table,
a small, square question mark
wrapped in brown paper.
tape like a scar
over its edges.

when i finally did it -
knife in hand,
the room holding its breath -
it wasn't what i expected.

no severed hand,
no cryptic note
from a lover i never had.
just a jar.
plain, unlabelled,
the kind you'd use
for jam or poison
or something worse.

i stared at it,
the way you stare at a word
you've written so often
it stops making sense.
inside - nothing.
or maybe too much.

that's the thing about mystery, isn't it?
it thrives on your imagination.
i put the jar back in the box,
shoved it under the stairs,
where it could haunt
the spiders instead of me.

days later,
the cat's gone missing,
the fridge ticks in a different key,
and there's a sound at night -
like glass cracking,
or someone opening a door
they shouldn't.

i tell myself it's nothing.
but every time i pass the stairs,
i hear the box whisper:
*you'll look again.*

## graveyard games

it was her idea, the ouija board -
said it'd be "spiritual"
a word she used like vegan mayonnaise:
full of promise, completely tasteless.

the graveyard was her pick too,
midnight under a moon so dramatic
it might as well have been holding
auditions
for the next werewolf flick.
she lit candles,
set the board on a tombstone,
and told me to be serious.

"spirits of the dead" she began,
voice like she was ordering gluten-free
pizza.
"are you here with us tonight?"

i couldn't resist.
my finger nudged the planchette.

y. o. u.

her breath caught.

"me?" she whispered,

like she hadn't studied theatre in uni.

she asked again,

"what do you want from us?"

i pushed harder this time:

a. k. i. s. s.

she pulled her hand back.

"kiss?" she hissed.

"oh my god, you moved it!"

"i didn't" i lied,

knowing full well the spirits were

probably rolling their collective eyes.

"spirits don't flirt" she snapped,

snuffing out a candle.

"this is serious"

i wanted to say, *you brought me here.*

instead, i spelled:

l. o. v. e.

because apparently, i'm tragic.

she glared,

hands off the board now,

arms crossed like a final act curtain.

"this isn't tinder" she said,

and marched off, leaving me alone

with the moon, the tombstones,

and a planchette that slid,

on its own this time,

to n. i. c. e.

because even ghosts

can't help mocking me.

**time alone**

time alone is the quiet engine,
the unseen cog that turns the self.
no voices, no glances,
just the ticking of your own breath -
steady, patient, enough.

it's the silence that untangles
the cluttered wires of the day,
a space where thoughts can stretch,
yawn, and find their proper corners.
in solitude, the world shrinks
to the size of your own hand,
its lines and scars familiar,
its weight just right.

alone, you can lean into the stillness,
hear the stories that whisper
beneath the surface of the noise.
you remember that you are not
the emails, the meetings,
the roles you juggle -

you are this,
this breath, this pulse,
this small, essential moment
of *being*.

it isn't selfish,
this quiet departure from the world.
it's the fuel you need
to return whole -
to give, to love,
to exist as more
than a scattered shadow
of who you are.

time alone is not empty.
it's full of the things
you didn't know you'd lost.
and in finding them,
you find yourself again.

**deathtrap in disguise**

let me tell you something about
rollercoasters.
they're not rides - they're *death threats on rails.*
"oh, it's fun" they say.
fun? you call strapping yourself into a
metal coffin
and being yeeted into the sky at 70
mph *fun?*
no, thank you.

first off, the queue.
thirty minutes of sweaty strangers,
kids licking the barriers,
and couples who think the line
is a great place to reenact titanic.
by the time you get to the front,
you've memorized every crack
in the concrete and questioned
all your life choices.

and then the seat.
the *tiny* seat.
who are these built for?
toddlers? supermodels?
not a grown man with a respectable beer belly
and thighs that could crush watermelons.
the attendant, always about 19 and smug,
pushes the harness down with a grunt
like they're compacting recycling.
"is it supposed to cut off circulation?"
i ask.
they just smirk and yank harder.

the ride starts.
clack, clack, clack up the hill,
and every *clack* is a reminder
that gravity is not a suggestion.
meanwhile, my brain's going,
"this is it. you've lived a good life.
mostly. well, you tried"
and then we drop.

you know what happens next?
i scream, but not in a cool, action-hero way.
it's more like a cross between
a panicked goat and someone
finding their browser history exposed.
wind slaps my face,
my stomach's doing choreography,
and i'm pretty sure i just swallowed a pigeon.

oh, and let's not forget
the *inverted loops.*
yeah, i love the sensation
of my internal organs rearranging themselves.
nothing says "good time"
like feeling your lunch defy physics
and head for the exit - both of them.

by the end, my hair's a disaster,
my dignity's somewhere on the track,

and my girlfriend's laughing so hard
she's crying. "you looked so scared!" she
says.
scared? no. *terrified.*
because i value my life, karen.

you want thrills?
go watch a horror movie.
jump out of a closet.
but don't expect me to sit on a glorified
catapult
and pretend it's entertainment.
rollercoasters are for people
with nothing to lose -
and clearly, i'm not one of them.

**sunday roast**

it starts with a spark of hope,
the kind that smells like rosemary
and hubris.
"this time" i tell myself,
"it'll be perfect"
the family's coming over -
the critics, the food snobs,
the *aunt who brings her own condiments.*

the potatoes rebel first,
burning their edges into blackened
protest,
while their insides stay stubbornly raw,
like me after a week of dieting.
the chicken - no, the *crown of the table,*
refuses to brown,
sitting pale in the oven like it's auditioning
for a zombie film.

gravy? oh, it exists.
a lumpy homage to my sad ambition,

clinging to the spoon like guilt.
and the yorkshire puddings?
more like yorkshire pancakes,
flat, sad,
whispering, "why bother?"

the smoke alarm joins the chaos,
screaming louder than uncle dave
when liverpool loses.
the dog eats half the bread rolls,
and the cat saunters across the counter,
leaving paw prints in the butter dish.

by the time they arrive,
i'm sweating like the broccoli i forgot to steam.
"oh, it smells... interesting"
my sister says, her smile sharper than
the carving knife
because a half-decent vet
could make the chicken cluck once again.

we sit down.
conversation circles around politics,
football, and *that thing i said in 2008.*
everyone eats,
because hunger is a great equalizer,
and by some miracle, no one dies.

afterwards, they pat their stomachs,
praise the meal with
"well, it's the thought that counts"
and leave with tupperware
of burned potatoes and guilt gravy.

i collapse in the kitchen,
staring at the wreckage.
next sunday?
they're getting a takeaway.

Printed in Great Britain
by Amazon